M000020112

Sisters

Sisters

A Celebration

RUNNING PRESS

PHILADELPHIA · LONDON

A Running Press Miniature Edition™
© 1997 by Running Press

Illustrations © Jackie Pardo/Arts Counsel, Inc.

Printed in China

Library of Congress Cataloging-in-Publication Number
96-71133
ISBN 0-7624-0111-7

This book may be ordered by mail from the publisher.
Please include $1.00 for postage and handling.
But try your bookstore first!

Running Press Book Publishers
125 South Twenty-second Street
Philadelphia, Pennsylvania 19103-4399

Contents

Introduction

Sister.

Love, hate, security, anger, comfort, and jealousy are all encompassed by that single word. The bond between sisters is like no other. While you love your brother, your relationship is fundamentally different. After all, he's a man. Your sister is more than just a friend and confidant, she's your reflection, a constant reminder of who you are and who you could be.

But your sister is more than just your mirror, she is also your closest companion. She's seen you at your worst and at your best. She's bossed you around, mothered you, tattled on you, and pushed every single one of your buttons.

Sisters

It was your sister's bed you ran to when you had a really bad dream. She brought you your homework when you were sick and let you cry on her shoulder when you were dumped by your boyfriend. Your sister stood up for you at your first wedding—the one you had in your backyard when you were five—and she held your hand through all of the real life triumphs and disappointments that followed.

Your sister knows you better than anyone else. No one else claims a shared history with you, as well as your bathroom, bedroom, and wardrobe. No matter how far away she lives, your sister is still the first person you call when you need a little encouragement.

Despite all your differences, you know that she will love you no matter what you do. She is closer to you than any other person in the world. She is your sister.

Getting
to Know
You

Sisters

I was eighteen months older;
eighteen months in which I
sometimes think I was waiting
for her, waiting for her to
be my friend and companion
against the parents.

Amanda Cross (b. 1926)
American writer

Getting to Know You

I stood on tiptoe
to look at her. She was big
for a new-born child
and had a wispy corona
of jet-black hair
so unlike the rest of us.
She looked very nice
sleeping peacefully
and I felt suddenly happy
to have a sister.

Jackie Callas
Greek writer

Getting to Know You

. . . at first, I saw no sister at all.
On peeping closer I saw a mass of
straight black hair surrounding a tiny
little face; she was fast asleep. I tried
to touch her but was gently pushed
back by Nurse Kite and told just to look.
This seemed to me to be an awfully dull
thing to do with a new sister.

Barbara Woodhouse (b. 1910)
English animal trainer

Sisters

Here was someone who would share, an equal. She would be treated the same as me. We were joined together by the nature of our sex. . . .

Joy Harjo (b. 1951)
American writer and poet

I think a sister's love
is idealized as
perfect, unshakeable.
We all want it, even if
we don't have a sister.

Lindsay Doren
American film producer

The desire to be and
have a sister is a
primitive and profound
one . . . It is a desire
to know and be known
by someone who shares
blood and body,

history and dreams,
common ground and
the unknown adventures
of the future, darkest
secrets and the glassiest
beads of truth.

Elizabeth Fishel (b. 1950)
American writer

With a sister, you learn to love and to argue, to share and to spar.

Dale V. Atkins
American writer and educator

When my sister
was born,
it was like losing
the garden
of Eden.

Adrienne Rich (b. 1929)
American poet

Getting to Know You

I can't imagine
what my life would have
been if things
hadn't been like this:
two pairs of eyes,
two female beings
taking measure
of each other's lives.

Kennedy Fraser
American writer

23

Sisters

How can you be a sister and not
know how else you might have been?
Mandy was smart, but was she
smarter? I was younger. She was
older. Braver. Taller. Stronger.
Sisterhood carries with it a sometimes screaming, usually silent "er,"
the "er" of relentless comparison.

Lisa Grunwald (b. 1959)
American writer

What happened
with them
made me happier,
made my life better.

Marilyn French (b. 1929)
American writer

My early childhood, I was told, was spent trying to hold my own against my livelier, stronger, and sometimes aggressive twin sister. She had mastered walking before I had, making her rounds in the crib by holding on to the railing. Barely able to stand on wobbly legs, all I could do was remain in one place, clinging to the railing. . . . Each time she encountered me during her exuberant rounds in this little cage, I was knocked down. Screaming and pulling myself up again, I was ready for the next push over.

Ilse-Margret Vogel (*b.* 1918)
German writer

Getting to Know You

We accepted our sisterly bonding as
"natural." It was only later when we
grew up and met other sisters who
were not close to one another, who
were bitter rivals, that we really
learned to value our bonding—
to appreciate it's specialness.

bell hooks [Gloria Watkins] (b. 1955)
American critic and essayist

*My sisters and I
were supposed to share
things . . . but we weren't
very good at that. . .*

Rosalind Russell (1911–1976)
American actress

She shared much with her sister. . . .
They had one bike and one sled
between them, and had learned long
ago that these possessions were not
worth the fights.

Ann McGovern (b. 1930)
American editor and writer

Sisters

**I was always putting
myself in my
sister's place. . . .
I substituted her feelings
for my own, and her
face for any face
described. Whatever the
author's intentions,
the heroine was my sister.**

Mavis Gallant (b. 1922)
Canadian writer

Getting to Know You

From birth to death, sisters model
and pattern their scripts on each
other's. They take cues from each other
about the way life is or might be, about
how to walk, talk, think, dress, about
what to fear and what to embrace,
about whom to like, whom to scorn,
about when to move and how far, what
to reach for and why.

Elizabeth Fishel (b. 1950)
American writer

Sisters examine
each other so
they can have a map
for how
they should behave.

Michael D. Kahn (b. 1936)
American psychologist
and educator

I know when I was nine,
feelings between my sister and
me changed. I became her
most loyal admirer, and
she became my staunchest
supporter. Still, most
relationships that have had

to weather nine years of
intense rivalry and resentment,
a few years of idolatry and
eight years of separation would
have dissolved long ago.
How did our relationship
survive these odds?

Anne Fishel

Sister of Elizabeth Fishel

There is space
within sisterhood for likeness
and difference, for
the subtle differences that
challenge and delight;
there is space for
disappointment—and surprise.

Christine Downing (b. 1931)
American writer

42

Getting to Know You

It's very interesting
to me that my
sisters are different,
because it makes
me know better how
other people are.

Florynce Kennedy (b. 1916)
American lawyer and activist

Sisters

You can't think how I depend on you, and when you're not there the color goes out of my life, as water from a sponge.

Virginia Woolf (1882–1941)
English writer
(to her sister, Vanessa Bell)

Natalie St. George, at sixteen, was at the culminating phase of a passionate admiration for her elder sister. Virginia was all that her junior longed to be: perfectly beautiful, completely self-possessed, calm and sure of herself.

Nan, whose whole life was a
series of waves of the blood,
hot rushes of enthusiasm,
icy chills of embarrassment
and self-deprecation, looked
with envy and admiration
at her goddess-like elder.

Edith Warton (1862–1937)
American writer

Sisters

We complain to each other
and about each other.
We have helped each other
sometimes and other times
wrestled with our inability
to help. We have been the
keepers of our continuity.
The people we can tell the
truth about our children.

Ellen Goodman (b. 1941)
American columnist

Getting to Know You

I don't know what I would
do without them.
I feel fortunate to have been blessed
with so many years of growing
to know my sisters. I only hope that
my two daughters will
share in that same sisterly love

Mimi Lennon (b. 1955)
American singer

I cannot deny that,
now I am without your
company I feel
not that I am deprived
of a very dear sister,
but that I have lost
half of myself.

Beatrice D'Este (1475–1497)
Italian noblewoman

My Other Half

What seemed inevitable
to me—so natural
it wasn't even questioned—
was this link between my
sister and me. . . . Who am
I if I am not my sister?

Patricia Foster
American writer and editor

Sisters

We know things about each other,
mostly through history,
from sharing the same closet,
the same toothpaste,
the same cereal every morning
for twelve years,
all the routines and habits
of being in the same family.

Amy Tan (b. 1952)
American writer

No wonder we feel so
close to this other woman
in our lives. No one knows
better than a sister how
we grew up, and who our
friends, teachers, and

favorite toys were. No one knows better than she the inner workings of our family, our parents' private and public selves.

Dale V. Atkins
American writer and educator

Sisters

I found myself thinking
of Lily and Margo.
They understood me.
I was always at my best
when I was with them
because they knew
what to look for.

Luanne Rice (b. 1955)
American writer

My Other Half

No one knows you
like a person
with whom you've
shared a childhood.

Alice Hoffman (b. 1952)
American writer

A sister is both your mirror— and your opposite.

Elizabeth Fishel (b. 1950)
American writer

When I dropped Rose
at her house, she kissed
me on the cheek.
The fact was that we had
known each other all our
lives but we had never
gotten tired of each other.
Our bond had a peculiar

fertility that I was wise enough to appreciate, and also, perhaps, wise enough to appreciate in silence. Rose wouldn't have stood for any sentimentality.

Jane Smiley (b. 1949)
American writer

Sisters

Siblings are important
because you know them the
longest. You will probably
outlive your parents and
you don't meet your friends
or your husband until later,
but your sisters are there
for almost the same time
that you are. . . .
they are just a given. . . .

Erika Duncan
American writer

We have always
been constant in
each other's lives.

Bennie Wiley
American businesswoman

Sisters

As the oldest sister in a
family of eleven, I guess
I could have felt very
overworked and over-
whelmed by the multitude
of diapers and bottles and
baby-sitting. But I never felt
burdened at all. My favorite
recollections are of bathing

chubby-bottomed toddlers,
cuddling a soaking wet
baby in bed with me in the
early morning, or just
rocking a new . . . sister.
My stability and security
was in and with my status
as "oldest sister."

Dianne Lennon (b. 1939)
American singer

Sisters

Between my sister and
myself things happened
naturally. . . . Her tears
were real, and if she
laughed at one of my jokes,
I knew she wasn't trying to
humor me. She alone
endowed me with authority;
adults sometimes gave in to
me: she obeyed me. . . .

Simone de Beauvoir (1908–1986)
French writer

Sisters

Every woman
has so many stories:
her own, her mother's,
her sisters'.

Marilyn French (b. 1929)
American writer

My Other Half

In time, I replaced Mamma when it came to reading to her. Eugenia . . . would curl up beside me and rest her small head on my lap, her long, uncut, light brown hair flowing over my legs, and listen with that dreamy smile on her lips as I read . . .

V. C. Andrews (c. 1924–1986)
American writer

I remember bathing,
feeding, diapering,
rocking, and hauling
Michie all over the place
until my little arms
would just give out. . . .
It was as if I were her

mommy and she was
my own little doll. . . .
From day one, Michie's
been more than a sister
to me. She is one of life's
absolute treasures.

Kathie Lee Gifford (b. 1953)
American singer and
television talk-show host

My Other Half

I give my sister a candle
from my cake and
feel proud when she pretends
to blow it out.
Or I point to the stars
in the black sky, and as
she looks up, I see them shining
in her dark eyes.

Karen Hirsch (b. 1941)
American writer

Scarlett turned smiling green eyes upon her younger sister, wondering how anyone could be so sweet.

Margaret Mitchell (1900–1949)
American writer

My Other Half

She pictured to herself
how this same little
sister of hers would, in the
after-time, be herself
a grown woman;
and how she would keep,
through all her riper years,
the simple and loving heart
of her childhood. . . .

Lewis Carroll (1832–1898)
English writer and mathematician

Sisters

. . . loving a sister is
an unconditional, narcissistic,
and complicated devotion that
approximates a mother's love. . . .
sisters are inescapably connected,
shaped by the same two parents,
the same trove of
memory and experience.

Mary Bruno
American writer

My Other Half

She lifted Lucía
and laid her head on her
shoulder. . . . She felt
Lucía's warm, deep breath
on her neck and it tickled
her. "Tomorrow," she whispered lovingly to her sister
as she entered the yard.
"Tomorrow I'll buy you all
the ice creams you want."

Helena Maria Viramontes (b. 1954)
American writer

You will never
truly know me
until you
understand
my sister. . . .

Catherine Deneuve (b. 1943)
French actress

We've lived together
most all of our lives, and
probably know each other better
than any two human beings on
this Earth. After so long,
we are in some ways like one
person. She is my right arm.

Sarah Louise [Sadie] Delaney
(1891–1995)
American dentist

My sister! my sweet sister!
if a name
Dearer and purer were,
it should be thine.

Lord Byron
(1788–1824)
English poet

. . . *so many sisters are best friends.*

Alexandra Stoddard (b. 1941)
American interior designer

Sisters

When she kissed my cheek
she whispered "sister-love"
in my ear, so softly
I wasn't sure I'd heard it
until I looked in her eyes.

Jewelle Gomez (b. 1948)
American writer

Friends for Life

That winter I'd wanted to fail
a subject just so I could hang back,
stay there with her, the two of us
walking around the drafty house
in sweatshirts and wool socks
and understanding each other
precisely. Bringing each other cups
of tea without having to ask.

Barbara Kingsolver (b. 1955)
American writer

Each year I resolve afresh
that my quota of aunthood
is full, that I no longer
am going to clutter my
head with new names,
new birthdays. But then

something happens, like finding in the mail another photograph of a new baby, and against my will they draw me in again.

Sara Suleri (b. 1953)
Pakistani-born American professor and writer

I have all kinds
of thoughts and
feelings about her,
but first and last
we are two kindred
bodies.

Kennedy Frazier
American writer

Sisters

In thee my soul
shall own combined

The sister
and the friend.

Catherine Killigrew (1530–1583)
English poet

The ashes we rise from.
Our words, the flame.
With our sisters
we make fire,
we dance in the glow.
Sisterfire.

Charlotte Watson Sherman
African-American writer

A sister
is a friend.

Kaonde proverb

I owe a great debt
to my sister . . .
she . . . helped me
to save my daily life
from silence . . .

Simone de Beauvior (b. 1908)
French writer

They had certain looks
they exchanged that
reminded them they knew
what was going on, and
trusted it would pass;
they had little routines,
murmurings, and
reminders of the day they

this and the night they
that. No one but family
could share those things;
they were too insignificant
even to mention to friends,
or expect that they'd
understand.

Rosellen Brown (b. 1939)
American writer

Sisters

For there is no friend
like a sister
In calm or stormy weather;
To cheer one
on the tedious way,
To fetch one
if one goes astray,
To lift one
if one totters down,
To strengthen
whilst one stands.

Christina Rossetti (1830–1894)
English poet

104

A ministering
angel shall my
sister be.

William Shakespeare (1564–1616)
English playwright and poet

Sisters

Often, in old age, they become
each other's chosen and most
happy companions. In addition
to their shared memories
of childhood and their relationship
to each other's children,
they . . . carry the echoes of their
mother's voice.

Margaret Mead (1901–1978)
American anthropologist

Friends for Life

My sister and I used
to joke about growing old.
. . . we would picture
ourselves many years and
several cats later,
fossilized into the barely
ambulatory creatures we
had assisted across city
streets in that distant past.

Elizabeth Kaye (b. 1945)
American editor

Friends for Life

Females,
beginning with my sisters,
had been my most loyal,
my most satisfactory

companions.

Luanne Rice (b. 1955)
American writer

Sisters

. . . I have already made plans with my sister Geraldine that if we are ever widowed we must live together in a house with several cats, although I don't like cats but it seems to go together.

Roseanne (b. 1952)
American actress and comedian

Friends for Life

From the time we were
babies Janet—just three
years my junior—and I were
the world's best pals. . . .
Janet and I have also
shared adult experiences,
both of comfort and
discomfort. Happy feelings,
or those of emotional pain,
have held us, strongly tied,
through many trials.

Kathy Lennon (b. 1943)
American singer

I remember slumber parties . . . where no slumber was involved, only secrets and dares. . . . I remember lunches that I never wanted to end. Birthdays that glowed. From all those times, those eternal sacred moments of my life strung together inside me, pearl by pearl, I learned what it is to be happy.

Michele Weldon
American journalist

Sisters

The two sisters
were always so happy
to see each other, sharing
among themselves
memories and stories
of their days on the farm
in West Texas.

Denise Chávez (b. 1948)
American professor, playwright,
and actress

. . . one's sister is a part of one's essential self, an eternal presence of one's heart and soul and memory.

Susan Cahill (b. 1940)
American writer

Friends for Life

The tie of a sister
is near and dear indeed,
and I think a certain
harshness in her powerful
and peculiar character
only makes me
cling to her more . . .

Charlotte Brontë (1816–1855)
English writer

To have a loving
relationship with a sister is
not simply to have
a buddy or confidante—
it is to have a soul mate
for life.

Victoria Secunda (b. 1939)
American writer

In the archaeology of our
existence, a childhood layer
remains: the pair of us lying
side by side on the grassy
earth in a tent and trying
to be brave enough to sleep.

Or huddled in the back
seat of the family car,
singing in girlish voices or
mute with the misery of the
motion-sickness.

Kennedy Fraser
American writer

Sisters

My sisters and I stand,

arms around each other . . .

and although we don't speak,

I know we all see it:

Together we look like our mother.

Her same eyes,

her same mouth . . .

Amy Tan (b. 1952)
American writer

This book has been bound
using handcraft methods,
and Smyth-sewn to ensure durability.

The dust jacket and interior
were designed by Maria Taffera Lewis.

The dust jacket and interior
were illustrated by Jackie Pardo.

The introduction was written
by Janet Mello Wetherbee.

The text was edited
by Elaine Mello Bucher.

The text was set in Wendy and Novarese.